FORCES IN MOTION

FAST AND SLOW

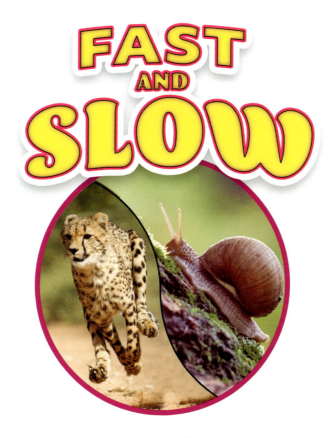

by Spencer Brinker

Consultant: Beth Gambro
Reading Specialist, Yorkville, Illinois

Minneapolis, Minnesota

Teaching Tips

Before Reading

- Look at the cover of the book. Discuss the picture and the title.
- Ask readers to brainstorm a list of what they already know about speed. What can they expect to see in this book?
- Go on a picture walk, looking through the pictures to discuss vocabulary and make predictions about the text.

During Reading

- Read for purpose. Encourage readers to think about when things go fast or slow as they are reading.
- Ask readers to look for the details of the book. What are they learning about forces that make things slower or faster?
- If readers encounter an unknown word, ask them to look at the sounds in the word. Then, ask them to look at the rest of the page. Are there any clues to help them understand?

After Reading

- Encourage readers to pick a buddy and reread the book together.
- Ask readers to name three things from the book. Do they go fast or slow? Find the pages that tell about these things.
- Ask readers to write or draw something they learned about speed.

Credits: Cover and title, © Kylbabka/shutterstock, © StuPorts/iStock; 3, © GlobalP/iStock; 4, © ManOnTheGo/iStock; 5, © Pentium5/shutterstock; 6,7, © THEPALMER/Getty; 7, © SDI Productions/iStock; 8,9, © inray27/shutterstock; 10,11, © Olga Oliva/shutterstock; 13, © Sasiistock/iStock; 14,15, © FatCamera/iStock; 17, © FocusStocker/shutterstock; , © Nirian/iStock; 18, © undefined undefined/iStock; 20,21, © kokoroyuki/iStock; 22T, © FamVeld/shutterstock; 22M, © NcikName/shutterstock; 22B, © Mega Pixel/shutterstock, © ho ura/iStock; 23TL, © anek.soowannaphoom/shutterstock; 23TR, © wavebreakmedia/shutterstock; 23BL, © FamVeld/iStock; 23BM, © Capuski/iStock; 23BR, © OlegRi/shutterstock.

Library of Congress Cataloging-in-Publication Data

Names: Brinker, Spencer, author.
Title: Fast and slow / by Spencer Brinker.
Description: Bearcub books. | Minneapolis, Minnesota : Bearport Publishing
   Company, [2022] | Series: Forces in motion | Includes bibliographical
   references and index.
Identifiers: LCCN 2021045037 (print) | LCCN 2021045038 (ebook) | ISBN
   9781636914107 (library binding) | ISBN 9781636914152 (paperback) | ISBN
   9781636914206 (ebook)
Subjects: LCSH: Motion--Juvenile literature. | Speed--Juvenile literature.
Classification: LCC QC133.5 .B75 2022 (print) | LCC QC133.5 (ebook) | DDC
   531/.11--dc23
LC record available at https://lccn.loc.gov/2021045037
LC ebook record available at https://lccn.loc.gov/2021045038

Copyright © 2022 Bearport Publishing Company. All rights reserved. No part of this publication may be reproduced in whole or in part, stored in any retrieval system, or transmitted in any form or by any means, electronic, mechanical, photocopying, recording, or otherwise, without written permission from the publisher.

For more information, write to Bearport Publishing, 5357 Penn Avenue South, Minneapolis, MN 55419. Printed in the United States of America.

Contents

Look at It Move! 4

Moving Fast or Slow 22

Glossary 23

Index 24

Read More 24

Learn More Online 24

About the Author 24

Look at It Move!

Look at that rabbit go!

It is very fast.

The turtle behind it is slow.

There are many ways to move.

Motion is when something moves.

A school bus moves on the road.

Your hand moves when you wave.

All motion is not the same.

It can happen at different **speeds**.

Birds are fast in the sky.

But clouds may go by slowly.

Your friend is swinging.

But she is going so slowly.

How can you help her move faster?

You can push your friend to help!

Pushing is a **force** that can change motion.

It gives your friend **energy** to go.

Now, she moves fast.

Pulling can change motion, too.

Your friends on a sled are not moving.

You can pull them!

Soon, they are zooming across the snow.

A ball rolls fast down a hill.

But how does this happen?

A force you cannot see is pulling it down!

This force is called **gravity**.

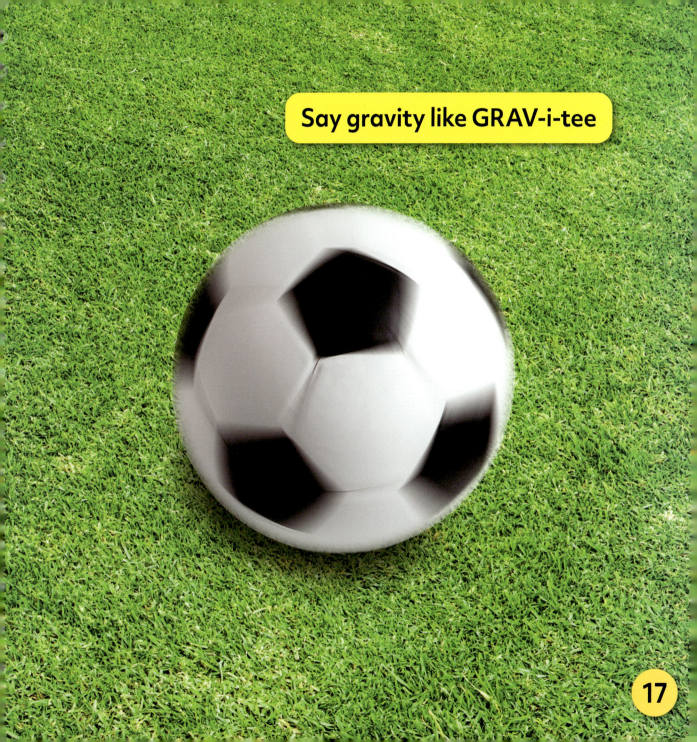

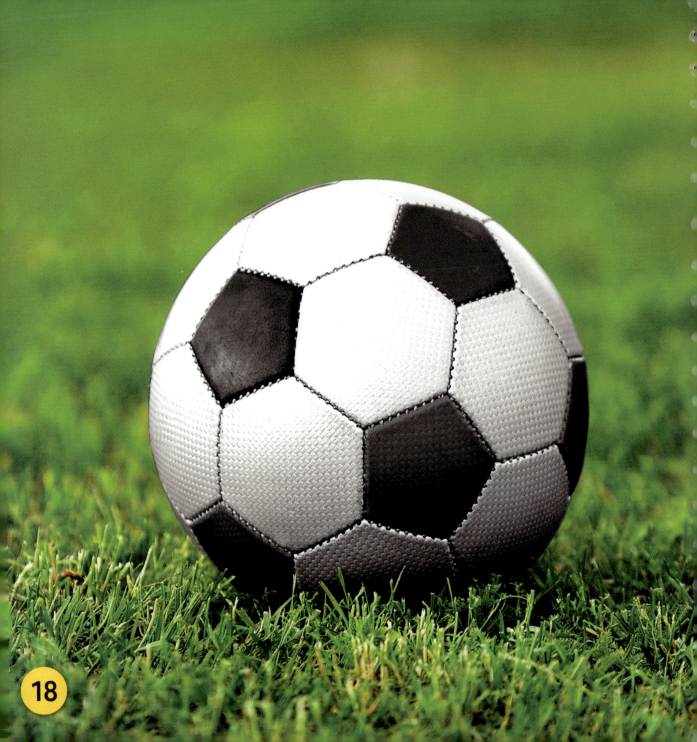

At the end of the hill, the ball is slower.

The ground rubs the ball when it moves.

This rubbing is a force that slows the ball.

Do you want the ball to go fast again?

Kick it hard.

This gives it lots of energy.

Look at it go!

Moving Fast or Slow

Some things move very fast. Other things move very slow. Let's take a look!

When you hit a tennis ball, it flies through the air. A strong force makes it go fast.

A leaf can float on the water. A little wind pushes it slowly.

A ball rolling on a small hill moves slowly. On a big hill, it goes fast!

22

Glossary

energy a measurement of how much work something can do

force a push or pull that makes things move

gravity a force that pulls things to Earth

motion the act or process of changing place or position

speeds quickness in movement

Index

energy 12, 20
force 12–13, 16, 19, 22
gravity 16
motion 6, 8, 12, 14
pull 14, 16
push 12, 22
speed 8

Read More

Duling, Kaitlyn. *Fast and Slow (My Physical Science Library).* North Mankato, MN: Rourke Educational Media, 2020.

Murray, Julie. *Fast and Slow (Opposites).* Minneapolis: Abdo Kids, 2019.

Learn More Online

1. Go to **www.factsurfer.com** or scan the QR code below.
2. Enter "**Fast and Slow**" into the search box.
3. Click on the cover of this book to see a list of websites.

About the Author

Spencer Brinker lives in Minnesota with his family. Sometimes their dog, Linzer, is fast, and sometimes he's slow.